11+
VERBAL REASONING

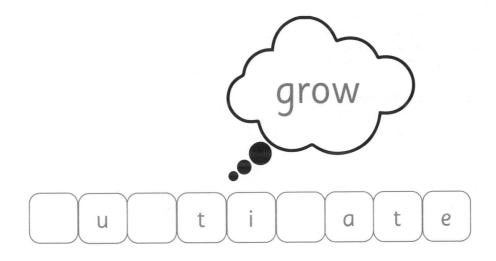

Ages 10–11

Practice

Series editor Tracey Phelps,
the 11+ tutor with a

96% PASS RATE

SCHOLASTIC

Published in the UK by Scholastic Education, 2020

Book End, Range Road, Witney, Oxfordshire, OX29 0YD

A division of Scholastic Limited

London – New York – Toronto – Sydney – Auckland

Mexico City – New Delhi – Hong Kong

SCHOLASTIC and associated logos are trademarks and/or registered trademarks of Scholastic Inc.

www.scholastic.co.uk

© 2020 Scholastic Limited

1 2 3 4 5 6 7 8 9   0 1 2 3 4 5 6 7 8 9

British Library Cataloguing-in-Publication Data

A catalogue record for this book is available from the British Library.

ISBN 978-1407-18377-0

Printed and bound by Ashford Colour Press

Papers used by Scholastic Limited are made from wood grown in sustainable forests.

Author

Tracey Phelps

Editorial team

Rachel Morgan, Suzanne Holloway, Audrey Stokes, Vicki Yates Sarah Davies, Julia Roberts

Design team

Dipa Mistry and Andrea Lewis

Acknowledgements

p43: Extract from *The Insidious Dr Fu* by Sax Rohmer; Extract adapted from *The Railway Children* by Edith Nesbit © Scholastic Classics; p44 Extract from Scholastic Close Reading Age 11+ © Scholastic Ltd; Extract from Mr Deane Goes Missing © Scholastic Ltd; p45: Extract from *The Great Mouse Plot* by Roald Dahl; p46 Extract from *Bosom Friends* by Angela Brazil; Extract from Scholastic Close Reading Age 11+ © Scholastic Ltd; p47 Extracts from The Pied Piper of Hamelin © Scholastic Ltd; p48 Extract from Gulliver's Travels © Scholastic Ltd; Extract from Scholastic Close Reading Age 11+ © Scholastic Ltd.

Contents

About the CEM Test

About the CEM test

The Centre for Evaluation and Monitoring (CEM) is one of the leading providers of the tests that grammar schools use in selecting students at 11+. The CEM test assesses a student's ability in Verbal Reasoning, Non-Verbal Reasoning, English and Mathematics. Pupils typically take the CEM test at the start of Year 6.

Students answer multiple-choice questions and record their answers on a separate answer sheet. This answer sheet is then marked via OMR (Optical Mark Recognition) scanning technology.

The content and question type may vary slightly each year. The English and Verbal Reasoning components have included synonyms, antonyms, word associations, shuffled sentences, cloze (gap fill) passages and comprehension questions.

The Mathematics and Non-Verbal Reasoning components span the Key Stage 2 mathematics curriculum, with emphasis on worded problems. It is useful to note that the CEM test does include mathematics topics introduced at Year 6, such as ratio, proportion and probability.

The other main provider of such tests is GL Assessment. The GLA test assesses the same subjects as the CEM test and uses a multiple-choice format.

About this book

Scholastic 11+ Verbal Reasoning for the CEM Test is part of the Pass Your 11+ series and offers authentic multiple-choice practice activities.

This book offers:

- Targeted practice and opportunities for children to test their understanding and develop their verbal reasoning skills.

- Opportunities to master different question types including cloze, spelling, vocabulary, synonyms, antonyms and more.

- Multiple-choice questions that reflect the different question types that are common in the

- CEM 11+ test, at a level appropriate for the age group.

- Short answers at the end of the book.

- Extended answers online with useful explanations at **www.scholastic.co.uk/pass-your-11-plus/extras** or via the QR code opposite.

Spelling

In the following sentences there are some spelling mistakes. On each line there is either one mistake or no mistakes. Find the group of words with the mistake in it and circle the letter. If there are no mistakes, circle the **N** in the box on the right.

1 There was no return adress on the back of the brown envelope.
A   B   C   D   N

2 Paul's mum had to email the school office to explain her son's absense.
A   B   C   D   N

3 Maisie's maths teacher was beginning to notice definate signs of improvement.
A   B   C   D   N

4 The weather was extremely changable throughout the whole of July.
A   B   C   D   N

5 Although not completely disasterous, it was still disappointing to have lost the match.
A   B   C   D   N

6 Although not proven, there are many people who believe in the existance of unicorns.
A   B   C   D   N

7 Neil's granny found detective novels particularly fascinating.
A   B   C   D   N

8 Ahmed wasn't ever frightened by thunder, but he was scared of lightening.
A   B   C   D   N

9 Although not strictly neccessary, the students were all asked to bring sandwiches.
A   B   C   D   N

10 One of the world's most famous playrights is William Shakespeare.
A   B   C   D   N

11 Clare fried potatos and bacon and served them with crusty bread.
A   B   C   D   N

12 Kieran's father was a professer of mathematics at Cambridge University.
A   B   C   D   N

13 Mateo couldn't decide wether he wanted to go bowling or watch a movie.
A   B   C   D   N

/13

14 Sophie had to seperate the egg yolks from the white in her cake recipe.

A	B	C	D

N

15 Gary had a huge arguement with his neighbour when he chopped a tree down.

A	B	C	D

N

16 Salma volanteered to work in a charity bookshop every Sunday afternoon.

A	B	C	D

N

17 The temperature had dropped to several degrees below zero overnight.

A	B	C	D

N

18 Max forgot to take any towles with him for his school residential trip.

A	B	C	D

N

19 Unfortunately, there is no garantee that there will be snow at Christmas.

A	B	C	D

N

20 It is an excellent idea to take proper advise before buying a new computer.

A	B	C	D

N

21 You can usually find the milk and cheese in the dairy isle in the supermarket.

A	B	C	D

N

22 Charlie chose all his birthday presents from a colourful catalog.

A	B	C	D

N

23 Trisha used her langauge skills to translate the speech from the Chinese politician.

A	B	C	D

N

24 Sofia was delighted to recieve an exquisite bracelet for her 18th birthday.

A	B	C	D

N

25 Howard Carter discovered the hidden tomb of the pharaoh in the Valley of the Kings.

A	B	C	D

N

26 Patrick's latest novel is based on the humourous diary of a boy who travels in space.

A	B	C	D

N

27 Mary's casual outfit was vastly inappropiate for such a formal occasion.

A	B	C	D

N

28 The concert had to be cancelled due to unforeseen circumstances.

A	B	C	D

N

29 Tala bought lots of miniture furniture for her new dolls' house.

A	B	C	D

N

/16

30 Noah was browsing through magazines to find himself a new hairstyle.

| A | B | C | D |

N

31 There are no penguins at the North Pole; they live and breed in the Antartic.

| A | B | C | D |

N

32 Some species of insects camoflage themselves in order to deceive their predators.

| A | B | C | D |

N

33 The trouble began when police charged at a crowd of unruly demonstrators.

| A | B | C | D |

N

34 Mahin kept interupting when his mother was admonishing him for being untidy.

| A | B | C | D |

N

35 Joe's cat likes to sharpen her claws on the legs of their dining room table.

| A | B | C | D |

N

36 Levi visited a bizarre to buy his groceries while he was in Morocco on holiday.

| A | B | C | D |

N

37 Puppies are expected to be quiet and obediant during their training classes.

| A | B | C | D |

N

38 The school governors reccommended that classes finish after lunch on Fridays.

| A | B | C | D |

N

39 Martha had a tight and hectic shedule and had to complete everything by noon.

| A | B | C | D |

N

40 Zac was in a very bad mood at dinner and wasn't being very communicative.

| A | B | C | D |

N

41 Arjun was excluded from attending school due to his previous bad behavour.

| A | B | C | D |

N

42 Anne phoned the restaurant to book a table, but there were none availible.

| A | B | C | D |

N

43 The team had already conceded two goals in the first three minutes of the match.

| A | B | C | D |

N

44 The spectators were requested to take their seats as soon as possable.

| A | B | C | D |

N

45 The quick-witted pilot avoided a tradgedy when she landed her plane safely in a field.

| A | B | C | D |

N

/16

46 Leo took the trouble to prepare some delicous cream cakes for the occasion.

A	B	C	D

N

47 The chilly whether began in September last year; there were lots of cold snaps.

A	B	C	D

N

48 After carefull analysis, Steve decided that an electric car would be the best option.

A	B	C	D

N

49 Zara was not eligable to play in the under-12 football team as she was 14.

A	B	C	D

N

50 It was impossible to guage the amount of liquid that was in the barrel.

A	B	C	D

N

51 Lui wasn't sure of the exact ingrediants, but she knew she needed nuts in the recipe.

A	B	C	D

N

52 Simon wisked three eggs together before adding cheese to his omelette recipe.

A	B	C	D

N

53 Our little village shop has very convenient opening hours and sells most things.

A	B	C	D

N

54 Olivia knitted each of her grandchildren fluffy woolen jumpers for the winter.

A	B	C	D

N

55 Aron asked his son not to play his music so loudly but he wasn't very cooperative.

A	B	C	D

N

56 Nathan was embarassed to admit that he was responsible for breaking the jug.

A	B	C	D

N

57 Liana sincerly believed that it was much healthier to have a vegetarian diet.

A	B	C	D

N

58 Priya found the disgraceful antics of her neighbour to be completely unforgivible.

A	B	C	D

N

59 Several senior managers were involved in the expensive advertising campaign.

A	B	C	D

N

60 Cameron had to complete a grammer and punctuation test on the last day of term.

A	B	C	D

N

/15

Synonyms

Circle the word which has the most similar meaning to the word on the left.

1	**current**	logical	topical	typical	comical
2	**obligatory**	conventional	comforting	compulsory	constant
3	**chase**	peruse	pursue	praise	purge
4	**jubilation**	elation	excitement	sensitivity	shame
5	**genuine**	dynamic	realistic	romantic	authentic
6	**unreadable**	legible	illegible	ineligible	tangible
7	**affluent**	purposeful	pretentious	precocious	prosperous
8	**remedy**	amplify	clarify	rectify	modify
9	**shrewd**	astute	strict	soft	alert
10	**steal**	eject	eliminate	embezzle	elude
11	**engulf**	overthrow	overwhelm	overrate	overspill
12	**fascinating**	controlling	stunning	appealing	enthralling
13	**elevate**	shove	heave	hoist	haul
14	**plunge**	settle	release	plummet	pierce
15	**plump**	refined	rotund	robust	roused
16	**unsafe**	precarious	infectious	mysterious	cautious
17	**commemorate**	return	memorise	recommend	remember
18	**snag**	cutback	drawback	tailback	comeback
19	**annihilate**	emancipate	elaborate	eradicate	excavate
20	**pretend**	flatter	flourish	fortify	feign
21	**opening**	ultimate	initial	principle	primary
22	**repulsive**	wholesome	fearsome	loathsome	irksome
23	**huge**	massive	sturdy	tough	solid

/23

24	**abstain**	repeat	refrain	recline	recur
25	**rickety**	uneasy	uneven	unstable	unmasked
26	**energy**	volatility	vitality	vibration	victory
27	**heritage**	tapestry	artistry	ancestry	chemistry
28	**opulent**	lavish	lacking	liberal	lengthy
29	**disguise**	swaddle	deceive	defend	camouflage
30	**faulty**	diverse	defective	defensive	destructive
31	**troubled**	accepted	agitated	brightened	congested
32	**accelerate**	promote	revive	quicken	inspire
33	**schedule**	diary	record	note	itinerary
34	**soaked**	sedated	smoky	saturated	shoddy
35	**naive**	unfortunate	forgiving	ignorant	gullible
36	**twisted**	gnarled	fabled	crushed	dappled
37	**thrilling**	exhausting	exhilarating	existing	exploding
38	**biography**	memorial	memory	memoir	memento
39	**hurdle**	opening	obstacle	objection	offence
40	**suggest**	include	satisfy	nominate	negotiate
41	**omit**	exclude	exhibit	exceed	excel
42	**highlight**	illustrate	illuminate	imply	improve
43	**reason**	motion	mania	manner	motive
44	**kudos**	poise	parade	praise	pattern
45	**movement**	method	purpose	principle	manoeuvre
46	**frank**	faithful	forthright	finer	former
47	**opposition**	reassurance	reliance	resistance	reference
48	**border**	frontier	glacier	plot	centre
49	**excavate**	unfold	unlock	unveil	unearth

/26

50	**clear**	decent	evident	absorbent	current
51	**relic**	article	artefact	advert	album
52	**punctual**	plump	polite	prompt	passive
53	**mingle**	interfere	imagine	imitate	integrate
54	**serene**	perky	placid	plain	plush
55	**appear**	embark	endure	emerge	engulf
56	**annoy**	provoke	promote	persist	propel
57	**pastime**	history	hobby	hindsight	holiday
58	**sagged**	drooped	soaked	bulged	lapsed
59	**sly**	futile	furtive	fussy	fierce
60	**reprimand**	serve	scold	sever	shock
61	**abhor**	deprive	decide	decay	detest
62	**scatter**	disperse	dictate	disclose	discover
63	**unavoidable**	irritable	unexpected	inevitable	forgivable
64	**arrogant**	concerned	covert	conceited	cornered
65	**solitude**	insurance	isolation	integration	incentive
66	**strong**	heavy	homely	hardy	humid
67	**busy**	bogus	blurry	buoyant	bustling
68	**lukewarm**	taut	tepid	tender	tardy
69	**unidentified**	eponymous	famous	various	anonymous
70	**artful**	cunning	creative	candid	curious
71	**replenish**	repeat	rearrange	refill	reconcile
72	**nimble**	vigilant	hectic	fussy	agile
73	**rival**	associate	opponent	cohort	observer
74	**essential**	vital	vivid	brisk	virtual
75	**offspring**	siblings	nephews	children	parents

/26

76	**crest**	pit	peak	pitch	path
77	**coax**	pursue	panic	prepare	persuade
78	**gloat**	boast	fake	sling	triumph
79	**embellish**	adore	adapt	adorn	advance
80	**flummoxed**	decorated	admired	plausible	perplexed
81	**envious**	dubious	jealous	frivolous	ominous
82	**sanctuary**	reception	recreation	refuge	residence
83	**scuffle**	muddle	tussle	tangle	mumble
84	**memento**	diary	journal	text	keepsake
85	**meddle**	increase	infest	interfere	influence
86	**famished**	starving	saving	satisfying	savoury
87	**colour**	trace	pigment	tone	wash
88	**dappled**	scorched	separated	surveyed	spotted
89	**smart**	dour	dreary	dapper	dreamy
90	**abrupt**	sullen	sudden	sodden	soaked
91	**failure**	malady	malfunction	malpractice	misconduct
92	**storm**	breeze	draught	tempest	flutter
93	**wither**	shrivel	sanction	scoop	sense
94	**shy**	boastful	baleful	wishful	bashful
95	**stick**	accuse	adhere	alter	await
96	**decimated**	deserted	haunted	obliterated	dedicated
97	**wholly**	exclusively	annually	politely	entirely
98	**tether**	shuttle	shackle	scorn	scribe
99	**haphazard**	dangerous	cluttered	accidental	random
100	**acclimatise**	adjust	acclaim	adopt	afford

/25

Antonyms

Circle the word which has the most opposite meaning to the word on the left.

1	**dismiss**	accuse	accept	attack	applaud
2	**construct**	replenish	diminish	establish	demolish
3	**anxiety**	control	composure	stability	simplicity
4	**healthy**	active	able	ailing	aged
5	**ludicrous**	incredible	sensible	terrible	gullible
6	**prohibit**	authorise	agree	appoint	adorn
7	**anguish**	contempt	control	courage	contentment
8	**blossom**	saunter	stalk	shrivel	stride
9	**slapdash**	formal	orderly	direct	earnest
10	**agitated**	talkative	tattered	tranquil	trained
11	**obedient**	sarcastic	scruffy	solitary	stubborn
12	**impolite**	courteous	cagey	capable	consistent
13	**decrease**	anoint	expand	unravel	simplify
14	**attract**	recur	renew	repel	reuse
15	**irritate**	pacify	parade	patronise	permit
16	**generous**	eccentric	miserly	modest	creative
17	**cease**	persevere	pierce	pester	plead
18	**active**	docile	doubtful	dramatic	dormant
19	**effortless**	graceful	grasping	generous	gruelling
20	**daunting**	revitalising	comforting	distressing	daring
21	**fascinating**	serious	tedious	humorous	fabulous
22	**sturdy**	fancy	feisty	fragile	flabby
23	**vengeful**	forgiving	forthright	forceful	forgettable

/23

24	**irate**	cagey	calm	curious	chic
25	**respect**	decline	delegate	demand	despise
26	**moist**	aged	arid	dusty	dreary
27	**careful**	tactless	restless	flawless	reckless
28	**frequently**	sparingly	seldom	gradually	slightly
29	**brief**	leisurely	light	lengthy	loose
30	**malicious**	harmless	thoughtless	relentless	tireless
31	**exhausted**	patriotic	ecstatic	artistic	energetic
32	**doubting**	resolved	convinced	intrepid	daunted
33	**pleased**	outdone	outraged	overawed	overwhelmed
34	**unexpected**	pondered	purposeful	planned	precise
35	**unappetising**	sweet	savoury	sour	scrumptious
36	**shortage**	selection	segment	surplus	source
37	**customary**	unusual	uncertain	unplanned	unrelated
38	**misunderstand**	believe	comprehend	include	imagine
39	**united**	integrated	deluded	divided	continuous
40	**waste**	consent	corrupt	compress	conserve
41	**apprehensive**	efficient	impatient	confident	competent
42	**release**	surrender	detain	prevent	excuse
43	**final**	basic	initial	lowest	main
44	**adore**	discard	discourage	disturb	dislike
45	**nourish**	starve	scare	scorn	stuff
46	**deny**	assist	claim	confess	challenge
47	**insert**	withhold	withdraw	withstand	overdraw
48	**inappropriate**	flattering	frustrating	fitting	furtive
49	**connect**	adapt	detach	despatch	shorten

/26

50	**agree**	qualify	quote	quench	quarrel
51	**continue**	tamper	thrive	transfer	terminate
52	**urban**	rural	regal	rich	ancient
53	**extraordinary**	natural	normal	neutral	needful
54	**cheerful**	dutiful	devout	dense	downcast
55	**spotless**	guilty	grumpy	grubby	gritty
56	**straight**	assorted	sorted	exported	contorted
57	**dull**	breathtaking	menacing	rambling	darkening
58	**safety**	custody	jeopardy	malady	parody
59	**fortunate**	unhelpful	unnatural	unlucky	unreal
60	**apparent**	unsatisfactory	uncovered	unclear	unpopular
61	**open**	secretive	defective	expensive	obsessive
62	**economical**	exhausting	extravagant	excellent	experimental
63	**meeting**	pairing	plotting	parting	posting
64	**deliberate**	conventional	fundamental	incidental	accidental
65	**variable**	constant	complicated	concerned	consecutive
66	**despatch**	research	reclaim	rescue	receive
67	**recall**	forgive	forget	forge	forsake
68	**content**	unhealthy	unethical	unhappy	unheard
69	**slow**	slick	swift	sluggish	slight
70	**reality**	frivolity	facade	fiasco	fantasy
71	**scarce**	beautiful	thankful	plentiful	needful
72	**aware**	illiterate	inexperienced	unable	ignorant
73	**deterrent**	imagination	indecision	impulse	incentive
74	**idolise**	deceive	detest	delight	demand
75	**fictitious**	factual	functional	fearful	fretful

/26

76	**flustered**	compliant	composed	coordinated	crinkled
77	**poor**	affable	affectionate	likeable	affluent
78	**fresh**	rancid	greasy	sour	bland
79	**unhealthy**	flavoursome	wholesome	awesome	fulsome
80	**clear**	ruffled	stuffed	shuffled	muffled
81	**dwindling**	informing	inscribing	increasing	inspiring
82	**lethal**	helpless	mindless	tireless	harmless
83	**disagreeable**	genial	arrogant	clever	flexible
84	**perfect**	faint	flawed	familiar	fictitious
85	**entice**	disburse	dissuade	disguise	dislodge
86	**compliment**	charge	cherish	criticise	contradict
87	**immune**	unqualified	unprotected	unhealthy	unnecessary
88	**plain**	ornate	elegant	simple	dainty
89	**ignite**	excavate	execute	exterminate	extinguish
90	**dapper**	shady	shiny	shifty	shabby
91	**fluctuating**	stretchy	stingy	steady	stocky
92	**compulsory**	alternative	optional	extraordinary	approximate
93	**vacant**	committed	pledged	involved	engaged
94	**juvenile**	sophisticated	mature	cultured	humble
95	**able**	inclement	innocent	incompetent	independent
96	**soar**	dismount	surge	descend	trickle
97	**lean**	stout	strict	spoilt	sublime
98	**first**	legitimate	duplicate	ultimate	fortunate
99	**lovely**	reluctant	redundant	refined	repulsive
100	**colossal**	brusque	miniscule	confined	crunchy

/25

Synonyms: missing letters

Complete the word on the right to have a similar meaning to the word on the left.

1 chaos   h [ ] [ ] [ ] c

2 decline   r e [ ] [ ] [ ] t

3 assessment   e [ ] [ ] [ ] u a t i o n

4 inferior   w [ ] [ ] [ ] e

5 end   c [ ] [ ] [ ] l u s i o n

6 contract   s [ ] [ ] [ ] n k

7 confused   b [ ] [ ] i l [ ] e r e d

8 unimportant   t [ ] [ ] v [ ] a l

9 defy   [ ] [ ] [ ] p o [ ] e

10 change   a [ ] [ ] [ ] d

11 dismal   d [ ] e [ ] [ ] y

12 swindle   [ ] e f [ ] [ ] u d

13 answer   [ ] e s [ ] [ ] n s e

/13

#	word	letters
14	reason	m _ t _ _ e
15	peak	_ _ m _ i t
16	sufficient	_ n o _ g _
17	ring	c _ _ m _
18	cure	_ e _ e d _
19	graceful	e _ e _ a _ t
20	lift	_ l _ _ a t e
21	altitude	_ e i g _ _
22	brook	_ t _ e a _
23	humble	_ o _ e _ t
24	foe	_ n e _ _
25	unoccupied	_ a _ a _ t
26	inside	i _ _ e r i _ r
27	grow	_ u _ t i _ a t e
28	rude	_ n s _ _ e n t
29	earnest	_ i n c _ r _

/16

Synonyms: missing letters

30	imitate	_ i m _ _
31	towering	_ o _ _ y
32	wilt	_ i t _ _ r
33	authentic	_ e _ u _ n e
34	qualified	s _ _ l _ e d
35	possibility	_ h a n _ _
36	excess	_ u r _ _ u s
37	mean	i _ _ _ n d
38	concentrated	_ _ _ t
39	wharf	_ a r _ _ u r
40	thoughtful	_ o _ s i _ e r a t e
41	extract	_ e _ o _ e
42	capable	_ o _ p e t e _ t
43	secluded	_ e _ o _ e
44	mistake	_ l _ _ d e r
45	saunter	_ _ r o l _

/16

46	dependence	r	e			a	n		e

47	speed		a	s		

48	combative	h			t	i		e

49	unreadable		l		e		i	b	l	e

50	harass		e			e	r

51	development		r	o		r		s	s

52	infamous	n				r	i	o	u	s

53	intuition	i			t	i	n		t

54	poisonous	t				c

55	notice	o		s		r		e

56	strong	r	o				t

57	result			t		o	m	e

58	delay	p	o				o	n	e

59	sly				n	i	n	g

60	beginner	n				c	e

/15

Antonyms: missing letters

Complete the word on the right to have an opposite meaning to the word on the left.

1 courageous   c o u r _ d l y

2 cease   c _ _ _ e n c e

3 reject   e _ _ _ a c e

4 allow   p r o _ _ b i _

5 reveal   _ _ n _ e a l

6 typical   _ n _ _ u a l

7 inaccurate   _ r _ c _ s e

8 real   i _ _ _ i n a r y

9 support   o _ _ _ s e

10 jeer   a _ _ l a u _

11 gather   s c _ _ _ e r

12 capture   l i _ _ r a t e

13 temporary   p e _ _ a _ e n t

/13

#	Word	Answer
14	lawful	i l _ _ _ a l
15	educated	_ _ n _ r a n t
16	boastful	h _ _ _ l e
17	absent	_ r e _ e _ t
18	fade	b r i _ t e n
19	unknown	f _ _ o _ s
20	hasten	d _ _ _ l e
21	receive	_ _ n a t _
22	calm	a _ i _ a _ e d
23	vile	p _ e _ s a _ t
24	hurried	l e _ _ _ r e l y
25	youthful	_ _ l _ e r l _
26	endless	_ _ _ m _ t e d
27	sturdy	_ r _ _ i l e
28	ascending	_ _ i _ _ i n g
29	purposeful	a _ _ _ e s s

/16

22   Antonyms: missing letters

30 change | p | | e | s | e | | | e |

31 loyalty | b | e | | r | a | | a | |

32 simple | e | l | | | o | a | t | e |

33 smart | s | c | r | | | | y |

34 clear | b | | u | | | e | d |

35 strict | | e | n | i | | | t |

36 jovial | | | | e | r | a | b | l | e |

37 guilty | | l | a | | e | | e | s | s |

38 abundance | s | | a | | | i | t | y |

39 abrupt | | r | a | | | a | l |

40 relax | t | | | | | t | e | n |

41 relegate | | r | | | | o | t | e |

42 installation | r | e | | | | a | l |

43 reluctant | | i | l | | | n | |

44 daring | c | a | | | i | | u | s |

45 gigantic | | i | | u | | e |

/16

#	Word	Letters
46	solid	h _ l _ o _
47	offspring	_ a _ e _ t
48	brief	l _ n _ t _ y
49	obscure	_ _ _ i o u s
50	neutral	b _ _ _ e d
51	impress	d i s a _ _ _ i n t
52	sparsely	_ e _ s e l _
53	plain	e _ _ _ o _ a t e
54	affix	r _ m o _ _
55	unsuitable	e l _ _ i _ l e
56	economise	s _ u a _ _ e r
57	decrease	a _ _ l i _ y
58	grim	_ l e _ s a n _
59	agree	c o n _ r a d _ c _
60	adjoining	d e _ a _ h e _

/15

Antonyms: missing letters

Synonyms: the odd one out

Circle the word which is the odd one out.

1	venomous	catastrophic	calamitous	disastrous
2	hanging	suspended	swaying	dangling
3	conquering	prosperous	victorious	triumphant
4	fearless	dauntless	intrepid	determined
5	grimy	soiled	dappled	dirty
6	repulsive	disgusting	disturbing	revolting
7	fatigued	fragile	frail	delicate
8	inflame	kindle	ignite	incense
9	fitting	adaptable	appropriate	suitable
10	misgive	misplace	lose	mislay
11	dawdle	linger	loiter	neglect
12	blemished	stained	patched	tarnished
13	seldom	scarcely	slightly	rarely
14	spring	swoop	plunge	dive
15	bolt	nail	sprint	dash
16	peril	jealousy	jeopardy	danger
17	develop	evolve	progress	diverge
18	melancholy	despondent	depressed	dismissed
19	wavering	hesitating	resolute	indecisive
20	thrive	furnish	flourish	bloom
21	dreadful	appalling	gloomy	ghastly
22	grief	sanity	sorrow	sadness
23	mimic	imitate	imagine	impersonate

/23

24	exhilarating	thrilling	exciting	trivial
25	diminish	dwindle	decrease	deteriorate
26	placid	serene	sombre	tranquil
27	embellish	garnish	drape	decorate
28	truthfully	candidly	cannily	openly
29	plentiful	copious	luscious	bountiful
30	positioned	situated	located	attached
31	insignificant	informal	trivial	unimportant
32	startle	stun	scare	soothe
33	pick	choose	allow	select
34	prominent	renowned	eminent	impressive
35	catch	grasp	swoop	grab
36	exceed	surpass	outstrip	survive
37	decent	impartial	ethical	righteous
38	compliment	commend	compose	praise
39	sleuth	detective	interpreter	investigator
40	ally	accomplice	collaborator	adversary
41	pilfer	steal	deceive	thieve
42	comical	funny	humorous	crazy
43	obliterate	destroy	demolish	decelerate
44	aggravate	prolong	irritate	provoke
45	extravagant	economical	thrifty	frugal
46	aim	point	intend	mean
47	disconnect	disengage	disarrange	detach
48	bright	smart	luminous	shiny
49	correct	rectify	accurate	exact

/26

50	beloved	dear	expensive	costly
51	adjoined	attached	adjourned	adjacent
52	disorder	distress	chaos	turmoil
53	careless	ruthless	spiteful	vicious
54	awkward	agile	clumsy	inept
55	knowledgeable	informed	observant	enlightened
56	hard	difficult	solid	firm
57	astonishing	incredible	amazing	improbable
58	instruction	teaching	order	command
59	triple	twin	triplicate	treble
60	permit	enable	allow	authorise
61	save	hoard	rescue	salvage
62	riot	rebellion	revolution	rotation
63	smart	neat	clever	astute
64	devour	gorge	feast	banquet
65	pursuit	chase	hobby	quest
66	perfume	present	fragrance	aroma
67	promising	prompt	punctual	timely
68	minimum	minor	lowest	least
69	idea	plan	concept	thought
70	harvest	festival	reap	gather
71	entice	attract	tempt	hoax
72	positive	certain	optimistic	hopeful
73	appeal	allure	request	plea
74	gift	talent	present	flair
75	answer	solution	response	reply

/26

76	totally	fully	wholly	exactly
77	sorcerous	dangerous	perilous	treacherous
78	lessen	dwindle	limit	ebb
79	wary	careful	cautious	certain
80	dribble	drizzle	trickle	surge
81	curious	enquiring	strange	inquisitive
82	desirable	detestable	pleasant	delightful
83	absurd	ridiculous	logical	nonsensical
84	effort	bother	disturb	hassle
85	probability	promise	likelihood	chance
86	bewildered	muddled	speckled	baffled
87	copy	drawing	duplicate	replica
88	follow	trial	trail	track
89	greatest	major	maximum	most
90	ban	prohibit	deprive	forbid
91	absurd	ridiculous	lucrative	ludicrous
92	purposely	deliberately	discreetly	intentionally
93	continually	constantly	alternatively	incessantly
94	mix	arrange	combine	blend
95	alter	mimic	change	modify
96	spot	stain	detect	notice
97	inept	astute	shrewd	canny
98	remember	recall	recollect	rectify
99	puzzle	riddle	anagram	enigma
100	mixed	assorted	united	varied

/25

Multiple meanings

Circle the word which has the same meaning as the words in both brackets.

1

[eat, nibble]			**[skim, scrape]**	
feed	chew	shave	graze	scratch

2

[reasonable, unbiased]			**[festival, fête]**	
fair	carnival	gala	trustworthy	honest

3

[make, compel]			**[strength, violence]**	
order	power	cause	force	energy

4

[summit, top]			**[badge, emblem]**	
height	peak	logo	crest	trademark

5

[stingy, miserly]			**[middle, average]**	
tight	ungenerous	mean	centre	core

6

[rubbish, trash]			**[deny, reject]**	
refuse	decline	debris	litter	spurn

7

[lessen, diminish]			**[deal, agreement]**	
shrink	pledge	contract	reduce	decrease

8

[shut, seal]			**[near, adjoining]**	
fasten	handy	around	lock	close

9

[arrive, alight]			**[ground, earth]**	
appear	soil	grass	stay	land

10

[straight, unswerving]			**[instruct, dictate]**	
direct	decree	command	undeviating	bearing

11

[good, great]			**[penalty, charge]**	
punishment	excellent	forfeit	fine	pleasant

12

[globe, world]			**[soil, ground]**	
sphere	earth	mud	planet	grass

13

[remove, withdraw]			**[excerpt, quote]**	
pluck	fraction	fragment	wrench	extract

/13

14	**[rapid, fast]**			**[armada, flotilla]**	
	swift	craft	fleet	liner	hasty

15	**[lecture, talk]**			**[residence, abode]**	
	dwelling	respond	appeal	address	housing

16	**[ordinary, middling]**			**[mean, median]**	
	fair	average	usual	medium	passable

17	**[banish, exclude]**			**[rod, pole]**	
	bar	reject	spoke	disallow	ingot

18	**[developed, created]**			**[calm, restful]**	
	formed	tranquil	constructed	moderate	composed

19	**[rule, custom]**			**[meeting, committee]**	
	habit	gathering	collection	convention	pattern

20	**[glow, brilliance]**			**[frown, scowl]**	
	brightness	grimace	glower	glare	gleam

21	**[chase, stalk]**			**[path, track]**	
	lane	follow	trail	route	road

22	**[hang, dangle]**			**[postpone, delay]**	
	pause	hinder	suspend	swing	shelve

23	**[relations, relatives]**			**[species, type]**	
	family	kind	sort	group	category

24	**[force, push]**			**[chunk, block]**	
	shove	portion	squeeze	hunk	wedge

25	**[cabin, chalet]**			**[stay, reside]**	
	villa	remain	board	lodge	cottage

26	**[bright, sunny]**			**[obvious, plain]**	
	pleasant	shining	evident	clear	visible

27	**[shore, beach]**			**[drift, cruise]**	
	bank	sail	seashore	meander	coast

28	**[call, phone]**			**[circle, loop]**	
	dial	band	ring	contact	round

29	**[sprint, rush]**			**[manage, organise]**	
	supervise	dash	oversee	run	dart

/16

30	[phantom, ghost]			[energy, enthusiasm]		
	desire	mood	demon	spirit	attitude

31	[end, tail]			[breed, raise]		
	back	rear	behind	type	elevate

32	[crumb, morsel]			[row, fight]		
	bite	bit	brawl	clash	scrap

33	[game, contest]			[alike, identical]		
	competition	match	fit	same	tournament

34	[frustrate, confound]			[rush, sprint]		
	dash	challenge	hasten	shatter	disappoint

35	[dismiss, fire]			[bag, pouch]		
	blaze	discharge	sack	satchel	flame

36	[prominent, strong]			[brave, fearless]		
	striking	daring	bold	vivid	gallant

37	[gale, breeze]			[screw, twist]		
	puff	blow	spiral	turn	wind

38	[argue, quarrel]			[paddle, punt]		
	pull	oar	row	quibble	feud

39	[lively, awake]			[signal, alarm]		
	alert	active	sharp	shock	warning

40	[flock, group]			[cram, fill]		
	herd	pack	squeeze	crush	stuff

41	[company, business]			[stable, steady]		
	level	firm	solid	balanced	club

42	[skin, leather]			[conceal, shroud]		
	camouflage	cover	fleece	hide	fur

43	[darkness, dusk]			[misery, sadness]		
	murky	black	gloom	grief	despair

44	[trophy, cup]			[give, present]		
	prize	medal	award	donate	grant

45	[follower, supporter]			[cooler, ventilator]		
	admirer	blow	enthusiast	fan	backer

/16

46	**[ringlet, curl]**		**[bolt, secure]**	
	hair	swirl	key	lock	protect
47	**[number, figure]**		**[finger, thumb]**	
	shape	calculate	toe	hand	digit
48	**[pill, capsule]**		**[slab, stone]**	
	medicine	rock	tablet	ill	brick
49	**[increase, expand]**		**[apply, smear]**	
	extend	extent	spread	employ	swell
50	**[transparent, translucent]**		**[obvious, evident]**	
	opaque	certain	definite	clear	crystal
51	**[relax, doze]**		**[leftover, remainder]**	
	lie	calm	nap	rest	surplus
52	**[rescue, salvage]**		**[hoard, collect]**	
	release	save	gather	assemble	free
53	**[slip, stumble]**		**[excursion, journey]**	
	fall	outing	trip	lurch	tour
54	**[teach, guide]**		**[order, command]**	
	educate	instruct	train	direct	coach
55	**[difficult, tricky]**		**[solid, firm]**	
	complicated	strenuous	stable	hard	rigid
56	**[scooter, motorcycle]**		**[frowned, sulked]**	
	scowled	car	bike	moped	glared
57	**[reason, justification]**		**[forgive, pardon]**	
	story	excuse	explain	spare	apologise
58	**[fib, falsehood]**		**[laze, rest]**	
	fiction	invent	lie	lounge	sleep
59	**[injury, cut]**		**[screwed, twisted]**	
	sting	damage	wound	turned	pinched
60	**[support, sponsor]**		**[rear, behind]**	
	raise	donate	tail	back	hind

/15

Multiple meanings

Synonyms and antonyms: the odd one out

Circle the pair of words that are the odd ones out; choose from the options A to D.

Example:

A	B	C	D
true, false	correct, inaccurate	authentic, real	genuine, fake

The correct answer is C, because all the other pairs of words are antonyms of each other. In option C, the two words are synonyms of each other.

1

A	B	C	D
strange, typical	unusual, abnormal	bizarre, odd	peculiar, weird

2

A	B	C	D
common, rare	amazing, stunning	amount, quantity	almost, nearly

3

A	B	C	D
bald, hairy	lofty, short	shy, bashful	scruffy, smart

4

A	B	C	D
critical, crucial	vital, key	important, trivial	serious, significant

5

A	B	C	D
pointless, futile	alarm, warning	disagree, quarrel	amusing, serious

6

A	B	C	D
examine, analyse	blunt, sharp	beg, scrounge	convenient, handy

7

A	B	C	D
awkward, graceful	short, brief	beaming, bright	breathe, inhale

/7

8	A	B	C	D
	cautious, unguarded	chaotic, ordered	savage, barbaric	praise, criticise

9	A	B	C	D
	wicked, evil	cruel, ruthless	honest, decent	disgust, delight

10	A	B	C	D
	scrap, snippet	pinch, whole	speck, spot	shred, sliver

11	A	B	C	D
	harm, injure	sodden, soaked	sprint, saunter	hazard, threat

12	A	B	C	D
	defy, disobey	delicate, fragile	accidental, intended	plunge, descend

13	A	B	C	D
	kill, slay	impartial, unbiased	calamity, tragedy	bright, dingy

14	A	B	C	D
	dodge, swerve	unite, separate	genuine, imitation	help, hamper

15	A	B	C	D
	doubtful, uncertain	endure, tolerate	gadget, utensil	expand, contract

16	A	B	C	D
	heed, ignore	frantic, fretful	real, mythological	informal, official

17	A	B	C	D
	drool, dribble	overhear, eavesdrop	emerge, vanish	ecstatic, elated

18	A	B	C	D
	concealed, visible	brisk, leisurely	sparkling, foaming	cheerful, morbid

/11

19	A	B	C	D
	reckless, responsible	interested, curious	plenty, insufficient	lethargic, lively

20	A	B	C	D
	possible, achievable	jagged, spiky	fake, forgery	forlorn, contented

21	A	B	C	D
	knowledge, wisdom	feasible, unlikely	ordinary, unusual	persuade, deter

22	A	B	C	D
	instinct, hunch	snub, insult	frequent, seldom	enrol, register

23	A	B	C	D
	placid, excitable	ultimate, last	pleasant, obnoxious	discourteous, polite

24	A	B	C	D
	coating, dusting	laughter, hilarity	hollow, solid	leaflet, pamphlet

25	A	B	C	D
	offended, insulted	docile, violent	usual, ordinary	thorny, prickly

26	A	B	C	D
	care, neglect	eerie, spooky	obedient, naughty	hopeful, pessimistic

27	A	B	C	D
	stab, pierce	practice, rehearsal	precious, cherished	omit, include

28	A	B	C	D
	necessary, optional	ready, unprepared	protest, approve	freedom, liberty

/10

29	A	B	C	D
	moral, shameful	emotion, feeling	pleasure, delight	mission, quest

30	A	B	C	D
	nervous, confident	proud, ashamed	detached, linked	scratch, graze

31	A	B	C	D
	publicise, advertise	derelict, neglected	extinct, surviving	surprising, startling

32	A	B	C	D
	occasionally, often	support, oppose	retreat, advance	lethal, deadly

33	A	B	C	D
	torrent, trickle	rhythm, beat	squander, waste	correct, factual

34	A	B	C	D
	punish, reward	sprightly, sluggish	adopt, reject	chase, pursue

35	A	B	C	D
	revolve, orbit	frivolous, sensible	scamper, scuttle	enthral, captivate

36	A	B	C	D
	agitated, serene	primitive, modern	assemble, dismantle	worsen, deteriorate

37	A	B	C	D
	routine, custom	fragrance, scent	generous, miserly	achieve, accomplish

38	A	B	C	D
	blurred, clear	struggle, grapple	conceited, modest	heckle, cheer

/10

Synonyms and antonyms: the odd one out

39	A	B	C	D
	heartless, ruthless	advice, guidance	hilarity, mirth	graceful, inelegant

40	A	B	C	D
	coarse, fine	jealous, envious	hesitant, decisive	endless, limited

41	A	B	C	D
	rotten, decayed	setback, snag	allowance, quota	insincere, genuine

42	A	B	C	D
	lank, bouncy	sombre, cheerful	carving, engraving	lenient, merciless

43	A	B	C	D
	insolent, impudent	stern, severe	magnify, decrease	alter, adjust

44	A	B	C	D
	prompt, punctual	unequal, level	lopsided, balanced	musty, fresh

45	A	B	C	D
	rumour, hearsay	tardy, early	shelter, protection	curious, intrigued

46	A	B	C	D
	neutral, biased	abolish, eradicate	influence, control	bendy, flexible

47	A	B	C	D
	accept, forfeit	pollute, cleanse	cause, prevent	ominous, menacing

48	A	B	C	D
	bulky, large	central, core	precarious, safe	compare, contrast

/10

Making words

Circle the word that, when added to the end of the word on the left, creates a new word. Choose from the options A to D.

1

page

A	B	C	D
and	art	ate	ant

2

bar

A	B	C	D
rears	ears	gain	rest

3

car

A	B	C	D
no	go	on	pit

4

fore

A	B	C	D
head	luck	round	tune

5

feat

A	B	C	D
them	her	him	they

6

is

A	B	C	D
lot	lit	line	land

7

leg

A	B	C	D
able	and	ally	idle

8

pan

A	B	C	D
the	there	try	tree

9

is

A	B	C	D
sue	sew	sea	hind

/9

10	of	A	B	C	D
		for	fence	fit	fur

11	for	A	B	C	D
		word	age	rest	teen

12	he	A	B	C	D
		ache	ate	arm	art

13	amen	A	B	C	D
		did	meant	able	ace

14	at	A	B	C	D
		tone	tempt	told	till

15	sea	A	B	C	D
		king	some	led	the

16	me	A	B	C	D
		and	ant	real	rent

17	refer	A	B	C	D
		rent	rant	red	read

18	rest	A	B	C	D
		tore	air	able	rain

19	no	A	B	C	D
		not	up	on	ton

20	arm	A	B	C	D
		my	met	amend	our

/11

21		A	B	C	D
port		tray	train	told	ray

22		A	B	C	D
temp		last	late	attire	pest

23		A	B	C	D
mode		darn	rate	ate	or

24		A	B	C	D
rot		test	ate	tend	are

25		A	B	C	D
rebel		lot	loss	less	lion

26		A	B	C	D
fort		teen	tune	night	right

27		A	B	C	D
pump		let	flat	kind	kin

28		A	B	C	D
pop		spies	peas	spaces	pies

29		A	B	C	D
so		at	up	or	be

30		A	B	C	D
overt		time	throw	took	urn

/10

31 the	**A**	**B**	**C**	**D**
	rest	me	airy	my

32 so	**A**	**B**	**C**	**D**
	in	of	on	an

33 was	**A**	**B**	**C**	**D**
	here	there	her	hold

34 sty	**A**	**B**	**C**	**D**
	lead	less	lad	led

35 all	**A**	**B**	**C**	**D**
	along	owed	together	in

36 mode	**A**	**B**	**C**	**D**
	late	dial	earn	sty

37 rein	**A**	**B**	**C**	**D**
	proof	coat	vent	drop

38 plea	**A**	**B**	**C**	**D**
	sent	used	sure	rule

39 disc	**A**	**B**	**C**	**D**
	continue	over	close	credit

40 off	**A**	**B**	**C**	**D**
	fend	ace	all	ice

/10

41	than	**A**	**B**	**C**	**D**
		key	more	king	led

42	kind	**A**	**B**	**C**	**D**
		art	lie	dread	led

43	reap	**A**	**B**	**C**	**D**
		peer	pair	pear	pare

44	no	**A**	**B**	**C**	**D**
		them	vice	veil	less

45	car	**A**	**B**	**C**	**D**
		pin	pen	rot	sty

46	tact	**A**	**B**	**C**	**D**
		full	less	turn	ices

47	steal	**A**	**B**	**C**	**D**
		maker	yard	worker	thy

48	rest	**A**	**B**	**C**	**D**
		tear	art	rein	tart

49	an	**A**	**B**	**C**	**D**
		either	other	neither	ever

50	arc	**A**	**B**	**C**	**D**
		way	hive	tick	aid

/10

Making words

Cloze passages

In the following passages, some of the words are missing. Complete each passage by selecting the words from the options A to H. Each word may only be used once. Write the correct letter in each answer lozenge.

Passage 1

A	B	C	D	E	F	G	H
framed	plush	carpeted	lit	occupied	glance	tidy	curios

Sir Harold's study was a small one, and a quick (Q1 _____) showed that, as the secretary had said, it offered no hiding place. It was heavily (Q2 _____) and over-full of Burmese and Chinese ornaments and (Q3 _____), and upon the mantelpiece stood several (Q4 _____) photographs. A map of the Indian Empire (Q5 _____) the larger part of one wall. The fire grate was empty, for the weather was extremely warm, and a green-shaded lamp on the littered writing table provided the only light. The air was stale, for both windows were closed and fastened.

Passage 2

A	B	C	D	E	F	G	H
belonging	delicious	which	fair	while	true	lucky	read

The three (Q6 _____) children always had everything they needed: nice, pretty clothes, (Q7 _____) meals and a lovely nursery with heaps of toys. They had a kind and merry nanny and a dog who was called James. They also had a father who was just perfect, never cross, always (Q8 _____) and always ready to play a game. The children's mother would play with them and (Q9 _____) to them and help them do their homework. She used to write stories for them (Q10 _____) they were at school and read out loud to them after tea.

/10

Passage 3

A	B	C	D	E	F	G	H	I	J
streets	damage	shock	turned	miserable	anger	hazardous	sounded	roofs	buckled

Winter began early this year and quickly (Q1_____) fierce. One storm after another kept the ground snow-covered throughout December. Freezing temperatures kept the (Q2_____) and pavements icy and dangerous. Not only driving, but walking, too, was (Q3_____). There were power outages and (Q4_____) from felled trees. Pipes froze and roofs (Q5_____) under the added weight.

Passage 4

A	B	C	D	E	F	G	H
punctual	prepared	curious	meticulous	dropped	creature	gathering	wonderful

Shelmore was a (Q6_____) of habit. He arrived at the office at exactly ten minutes to ten each morning, and at ten minutes to five each afternoon he (Q7_____) to leave it. He was preparing to leave it now on this unusually fine Wednesday in September, tidying his desk and (Q8_____) his hat, overcoat, umbrella and newspaper, ready for his departure. As he put on his gloves with (Q9_____) precision, he cast a glance out to the street below.

At that moment, something (Q10_____) caught his eye. A girl stood on the kerb, looking doubtfully and enquiringly around. She was tall, slim and smartly dressed. He wondered about her without knowing why he wondered.

/10

Passage 5

A	B	C	D	E	F	G	H
sweets	hollow	found	examine	four	lying	prised	five

My four friends and I had come across a loose floorboard at the back of the classroom, and when we (Q1) it up with the blade of a pocket-knife, we discovered a big (Q2) space underneath. This, we decided, would be our secret hiding place for sweets and other small treasures such as conkers and monkey nuts and birds' eggs. Every afternoon, when the last lesson was over, the (Q3) of us would wait until the classroom had emptied, then we would lift up the floorboard and (Q4) our secret hoard, perhaps adding to it or taking something away. One day, when we lifted it up, we found a dead mouse (Q5) among our treasures.

Passage 6

A	B	C	D	E	F	G	H
perspective	glance	finding	immense	interest	perched	observing	poised

Many who pass through this (Q6), majestic train station take an occasional (Q7) in my direction. I, meanwhile, have been (Q8) them all for years from my bird's-eye (Q9). I, you see, am an oversized clock (Q10) high upon the wall.

/10

Passage 7

A	B	C	D	E	F	G	H
travel	wafted	hearty	kind	circular	accompany	fashion	thoughtfully

The small girl was due to leave London that morning by the coach that stopped outside
the Houses of Parliament at 9am. Her father had been sent up to Scotland on business
and her Aunt Ruth would (Q1) her on the long journey. Aunt Ruth had
(Q2) turned on the fire to warm the room for Lilly and then proceeded to
make a start on preparing a (Q3) breakfast for her young niece.

When Lilly finally appeared downstairs, she seemed to be rubbing her eyes in a gentle
(Q4) motion. Aunt Ruth had made a concoction of porridge and fruit and
berries that morning and the aroma (Q5) through the kitchen.

Passage 8

A	B	C	D	E	F	G	H	I	J
instrument	asked	melodies	ignored	voices	fascination	concern	encouraged	bragged	cultivated

Alyssa Linton had always been a musical child. Her mother (Q6) that her
daughter sang before she spoke and that she picked out (Q7) on the family
piano before she ever took lessons. So it made sense that Alyssa (Q8) that
early (Q9) for anything that she could use to make music. Her voice was her
first (Q10). Then came piano, recorder and accordion.

/10

Passage 9

A	B	C	D	E	F	G	H
sugary	infested	besotted	found	banks	nest	gnawed	squeaking

Hamelin is a sleepy little town, spread out along the (Q1_____) of a deep, wide river. At one time, what made it an especially lively place was its rats: the place was so (Q2_____) with them as to be hardly worth living in. There was not a barn or cupboard that hadn't been eaten into; not a cheese that the rats hadn't (Q3_____) hollow; not a (Q4_____) treat that they hadn't gobbled up. The noise of rats hurrying and scurrying and (Q5_____) was so loud that no one in the town could get any rest.

No matter what they tried — cats, poison, rat-catchers, traps — every day there seemed to be more rats than ever. The mayor and the town council were at their wits' end.

Passage 10

A	B	C	D	E	F	G	H
paying	piercing	parting	news	willing	single	received	brought

As they were sitting in the town hall one day, a messenger (Q6_____) word that a strange man was at the town gates. This stranger was tall and thin, with (Q7_____) eyes. He wore a coat with all the colours of the rainbow, and he offered to get rid of the rats. "I'm called the Pied Piper," he began. "What might you be (Q8_____) to pay me, if I rid you of every rat in your town?"

Well, much as the town's leaders feared the rats, they feared (Q9_____) with their money even more. Nevertheless, they promised to pay the Pied Piper fifty crowns — a generous sum — as long as not a (Q10_____) rat was left to squeak in Hamelin.

/10

Passage 11

A	B	C	D	E	F	G	H
houses	town	conjectured	people	inclined	sounder	sand	advanced

I walked nearly a mile before I got to the shore; it was, I (**Q1**), about eight o'clock in the evening. I then (**Q2**) forward nearly half a mile, but could not discover any sign of (**Q3**) or inhabitants; at least, I was in so weak a condition that I did not observe them.

I was extremely tired; with that, and the heat of the weather, I found myself (**Q4**) to sleep. I lay down on the grass, which was very short and soft, where I slept (**Q5**) than ever I remember to have done in my life. I reckoned it was about nine hours, for when I awoke, it was just daylight.

Passage 12

A	B	C	D	E	F	G	H	I	J
understandably	irked	joyous	decision	terribly	enabled	enjoyed	focused	visited	wretched

Hunter frequently posts reviews of restaurants he visits. One day recently, he posted a review on his favourite dining site YUMM.com. He wrote this review:

'It was bad enough that Manuela's was (**Q6**) crowded and deafening, but the (**Q7**) food and second-rate service (**Q8**) us all. Since we could hardly hear what one another was saying, we all (**Q9**) on our food, which proved to be a disappointing (**Q10**).

Shuffled sentences

In each question below, the words may be rearranged to form a sentence. One word does not belong in the sentence. Circle the superfluous word from the options A to H.

1

tantrum	Jimmy	when	died	rabbit	his	pet	cried
A	B	C	D	E	F	G	H

2

slippers	Mavis	was	used	her	with	thrilled	new
A	B	C	D	E	F	G	H

3

tasty	make	lunch	very	bread	a	these	sandwiches
A	B	C	D	E	F	G	H

4

watch	fast	always	was	Marc's	minutes	ten	needs
A	B	C	D	E	F	G	H

5

history	times	invented	many	in	machines	Victorian	were
A	B	C	D	E	F	G	H

6

in	frog	water	and	land	live	on	amphibians
A	B	C	D	E	F	G	H

7

played	football	all	the	is	every	over	world
A	B	C	D	E	F	G	H

8

of	shelves	the	books	were	children's	full	mixed
A	B	C	D	E	F	G	H

/8

9

under	Bella	wishes	her	found	bed	some	comics
A	B	C	D	E	F	G	H

10

shark	intelligent	dolphins	and	are	highly	friendly	very
A	B	C	D	E	F	G	H

11

of	are	sometimes	can	be	works	art	priceless
A	B	C	D	E	F	G	H

12

people	in	certain	jobs	courses	wear	some	uniforms
A	B	C	D	E	F	G	H

13

winter	fluff	their	in	flutter	feathers	birds	up
A	B	C	D	E	F	G	H

14

diary	like	every	day	keep	people	a	some
A	B	C	D	E	F	G	H

15

foods	you	like	water	energy	bread	starchy	give
A	B	C	D	E	F	G	H

16

to	Romans	roads	baths	used	the	visit	public
A	B	C	D	E	F	G	H

17

builders	new	scaffold	are	homes	some	the	constructing
A	B	C	D	E	F	G	H

18

car	batteries	the	pollute	fumes	exhausts	from	air
A	B	C	D	E	F	G	H

19

safari	enjoy	on	Africa	you	in	can	go
A	B	C	D	E	F	G	H

/11

20

falling	it	air	parachute	traps	a	makes	underneath
A	B	C	D	E	F	G	H

21

China	food	rice	the	is	of	staple	tea
A	B	C	D	E	F	G	H

22

old	crumble	and	repairing	bridge	needed	was	the
A	B	C	D	E	F	G	H

23

Sam	her	games	borrowed	from	lent	some	brother
A	B	C	D	E	F	G	H

24

some	can't	a	people	secret	party	keep	really
A	B	C	D	E	F	G	H

25

milk	coffee	cereal	put	on	their	most	people
A	B	C	D	E	F	G	H

26

lawyer	Poppy's	airline	is	pilot	a	successful	dad
A	B	C	D	E	F	G	H

27

Blanca	football	team	every	training	week	goes	to
A	B	C	D	E	F	G	H

28

at	daily	weekends	library	opens	except	the	often
A	B	C	D	E	F	G	H

29

really	with	Amy	brother	her	liked	annoyed	was
A	B	C	D	E	F	G	H

30

delayed	an	was	bumpy	Bridget's	by	hour	flight
A	B	C	D	E	F	G	H

/11

31

poured	milk	spilled	a	Walter	of	glass	himself
A	B	C	D	E	F	G	H

32

paid	holiday	a	France	family	the	to	booked
A	B	C	D	E	F	G	H

33

to	his	needed	repair	Peter	car	want	old
A	B	C	D	E	F	G	H

34

was	tired	than	Alfie	his	taller	brother	much
A	B	C	D	E	F	G	H

35

among	village	sits	two	the	farms	church	between
A	B	C	D	E	F	G	H

36

in	windmills	the	countryside	was	common	once	were
A	B	C	D	E	F	G	H

37

boys	should	their	of	the	remembered	have	keys
A	B	C	D	E	F	G	H

38

sometime	must	over	come	you	love	soon	again
A	B	C	D	E	F	G	H

39

his	piano	key	Ajay	weekly	really	lesson	hated
A	B	C	D	E	F	G	H

40

cut	of	during	electricity	storm	a	out	the
A	B	C	D	E	F	G	H

/10

Shuffled sentences

41

has	her	exams	Izzy	is	well	done	in
A	B	C	D	E	F	G	H

42

were	we	running	of	cat	out	was	food
A	B	C	D	E	F	G	H

43

always	in	an	remained	crisis	John	a	calm
A	B	C	D	E	F	G	H

44

caked	were	absolutely	mud	the	with	a	wheels
A	B	C	D	E	F	G	H

45

for	to	had	run	the	I	bus	catch
A	B	C	D	E	F	G	H

46

difficult	made	fog	see	to	was	the	it
A	B	C	D	E	F	G	H

47

looked	road	over	he	and	the	up	down
A	B	C	D	E	F	G	H

48

socks	and	Diya	off	shoes	took	all	her
A	B	C	D	E	F	G	H

49

and	paid	no	friends	were	Jack	attention	his
A	B	C	D	E	F	G	H

50

has	built	the	they	sand	in	castles	had
A	B	C	D	E	F	G	H

/10

51	was	the	unaware	Matthew	danger	frightened	of	blissfully
	A	B	C	D	E	F	G	H

52	can	heights	rarely	scared	of	be	people	sometimes
	A	B	C	D	E	F	G	H

53	expensive	ought	in	can	be	very	London	hotels
	A	B	C	D	E	F	G	H

54	outside	Victorian	an	cold	toilet	houses	had	often
	A	B	C	D	E	F	G	H

55	were	on	the	fish	in	swimming	their	tank
	A	B	C	D	E	F	G	H

56	bills	winter	in	can	cold	be	electricity	expensive
	A	B	C	D	E	F	G	H

57	drinks	only	fizzy	healthy	you	not	for	are
	A	B	C	D	E	F	G	H

58	was	more	up	the	traffic	held	coach	in
	A	B	C	D	E	F	G	H

59	went	the	Lukas	doctor	his	visited	rash	about
	A	B	C	D	E	F	G	H

60	have	to	agreement	finally	an	a	they	come
	A	B	C	D	E	F	G	H

/10

Shuffled sentences

Answers

Spelling
pp.5–6

1	B	address
2	D	absence
3	C	definite
4	C	changeable
5	B	disastrous
6	D	existence
7	N	—
8	D	lightning
9	B	necessary
10	C	playwrights
11	A	potatoes
12	B	professor
13	B	whether
14	B	separate
15	B	argument
16	A	volunteered
17	N	—
18	B	towels
19	B	guarantee
20	C	advice
21	D	aisle
22	D	catalogue
23	A	language
24	B	receive
25	N	—
26	B	humorous
27	C	inappropriate
28	N	—
29	B	miniature

Spelling
pp.7–8

30	N	—
31	D	Antarctic
32	B	camouflage
33	N	—
34	A	interrupting
35	N	—
36	B	bazaar
37	C	obedient
38	B	recommended
39	C	schedule
40	N	—
41	D	behaviour
42	D	available
43	N	—
44	D	possible
45	B	tragedy
46	C	delicious
47	A	weather
48	A	careful
49	A	eligible
50	B	gauge
51	B	ingredients
52	A	whisked
53	N	—
54	C	woollen
55	N	—
56	A	embarrassed
57	A	sincerely
58	D	unforgivable
59	N	—
60	B	grammar

Synonyms
p.9

1	topical
2	compulsory
3	pursue
4	elation
5	authentic
6	illegible
7	prosperous
8	rectify
9	astute
10	embezzle
11	overwhelm
12	enthralling
13	hoist
14	plummet
15	rotund
16	precarious
17	remember
18	drawback
19	eradicate
20	feign
21	initial
22	loathsome
23	massive

Synonyms
p.10

24	refrain
25	unstable
26	vitality
27	ancestry
28	lavish
29	camouflage
30	defective
31	agitated
32	quicken
33	itinerary
34	saturated
35	gullible
36	gnarled
37	exhilarating
38	memoir
39	obstacle
40	nominate
41	exclude
42	illuminate
43	motive
44	praise
45	manoeuvre
46	forthright
47	resistance
48	frontier
49	unearth

Answers

Synonyms
p.11

50	evident
51	artefact
52	prompt
53	integrate
54	placid
55	emerge
56	provoke
57	hobby
58	drooped
59	furtive
60	scold
61	detest
62	disperse
63	inevitable
64	conceited
65	isolation
66	hardy
67	bustling
68	tepid
69	anonymous
70	cunning
71	refill
72	agile
73	opponent
74	vital
75	children

Synonyms
p.12

76	peak
77	persuade
78	boast
79	adorn
80	perplexed
81	jealous
82	refuge
83	tussle
84	keepsake
85	interfere
86	starving
87	pigment
88	spotted
89	dapper
90	sudden
91	malfunction
92	tempest
93	shrivel
94	bashful
95	adhere
96	obliterated
97	entirely
98	shackle
99	random
100	adjust

Antonyms
p.13

1	accept
2	demolish
3	composure
4	ailing
5	sensible
6	authorise
7	contentment
8	shrivel
9	orderly
10	tranquil
11	stubborn
12	courteous
13	expand
14	repel
15	pacify
16	miserly
17	persevere
18	dormant
19	gruelling
20	comforting
21	tedious
22	fragile
23	forgiving

Antonyms
p.14

24	calm
25	despise
26	arid
27	reckless
28	seldom
29	lengthy
30	harmless
31	energetic
32	convinced
33	outraged
34	planned
35	scrumptious
36	surplus
37	unusual
38	comprehend
39	divided
40	conserve
41	confident
42	detain
43	initial
44	dislike
45	starve
46	confess
47	withdraw
48	fitting
49	detach

Answers

Antonyms
p.15

50	quarrel
51	terminate
52	rural
53	normal
54	downcast
55	grubby
56	contorted
57	breathtaking
58	jeopardy
59	unlucky
60	unclear
61	secretive
62	extravagant
63	parting
64	accidental
65	constant
66	receive
67	forget
68	unhappy
69	swift
70	fantasy
71	plentiful
72	ignorant
73	incentive
74	detest
75	factual

Antonyms
p.16

76	composed
77	affluent
78	rancid
79	wholesome
80	muffled
81	increasing
82	harmless
83	genial
84	flawed
85	dissuade
86	criticise
87	unprotected
88	ornate
89	extinguish
90	shabby
91	steady
92	optional
93	engaged
94	mature
95	incompetent
96	descend
97	stout
98	ultimate
99	repulsive
100	miniscule

Synonyms: missing letters
pp.17–18

1	havoc
2	reject
3	evaluation
4	worse
5	conclusion
6	shrink
7	bewildered
8	trivial
9	oppose
10	amend
11	dreary
12	defraud
13	response
14	motive
15	summit
16	enough
17	chime
18	remedy
19	elegant
20	elevate
21	height
22	stream
23	modest
24	enemy
25	vacant
26	interior
27	cultivate
28	insolent
29	sincere

Synonyms: missing letters
pp.19–20

30	mimic
31	lofty
32	wither
33	genuine
34	skilled
35	chance
36	surplus
37	intend
38	neat
39	harbour
40	considerate
41	remove
42	competent
43	remote
44	blunder
45	stroll
46	reliance
47	haste
48	hostile
49	illegible
50	pester
51	progress
52	notorious
53	instinct
54	toxic
55	observe
56	robust
57	outcome
58	postpone
59	cunning
60	novice

Answers

Antonyms: missing letters pp.21–22

1	cowardly
2	commence
3	embrace
4	prohibit
5	conceal
6	unusual
7	precise
8	imaginary
9	oppose
10	applaud
11	scatter
12	liberate
13	permanent
14	illegal
15	ignorant
16	humble
17	present
18	brighten
19	famous
20	dawdle
21	donate
22	agitated
23	pleasant
24	leisurely
25	elderly
26	limited
27	fragile
28	sinking
29	aimless

Antonyms: missing letters pp.23–24

30	preserve
31	betrayal
32	elaborate
33	scruffy
34	blurred
35	lenient
36	miserable
37	blameless
38	scarcity
39	gradual
40	tighten
41	promote
42	removal
43	willing
44	cautious
45	minute
46	hollow
47	parent
48	lengthy
49	obvious
50	biased
51	disappoint
52	densely
53	elaborate
54	remove
55	eligible
56	squander
57	amplify
58	spotless
59	contradict
60	detached

Synonyms: the odd one out p.25

1	venomous
2	swaying
3	prosperous
4	determined
5	dappled
6	disturbing
7	fatigued
8	incense
9	adaptable
10	misgive
11	neglect
12	patched
13	slightly
14	spring
15	nail
16	jealousy
17	diverge
18	dismissed
19	resolute
20	furnish
21	gloomy
22	sanity
23	imagine

Synonyms: the odd one out p.26

24	trivial
25	deteriorate
26	sombre
27	drape
28	cannily
29	luscious
30	attached
31	informal
32	soothe
33	allow
34	impressive
35	swoop
36	survive
37	impartial
38	compose
39	interpreter
40	adversary
41	deceive
42	crazy
43	decelerate
44	prolong
45	extravagant
46	point
47	disarrange
48	smart
49	rectify

Answers

Synonyms: the odd one out p.27

50	beloved
51	adjourned
52	distress
53	careless
54	agile
55	observant
56	difficult
57	improbable
58	teaching
59	twin
60	enable
61	hoard
62	rotation
63	neat
64	banquet
65	hobby
66	present
67	promising
68	minor
69	plan
70	festival
71	hoax
72	certain
73	allure
74	present
75	solution

Synonyms: the odd one out p.28

76	exactly
77	sorcerous
78	limit
79	certain
80	surge
81	strange
82	detestable
83	logical
84	effort
85	promise
86	speckled
87	drawing
88	trial
89	major
90	deprive
91	lucrative
92	discreetly
93	alternatively
94	arrange
95	mimic
96	stain
97	inept
98	rectify
99	anagram
100	united

Multiple meanings pp.29–30

1	graze
2	fair
3	force
4	crest
5	mean
6	refuse
7	contract
8	close
9	land
10	direct
11	fine
12	earth
13	extract
14	fleet
15	address
16	average
17	bar
18	composed
19	convention
20	glare
21	trail
22	suspend
23	family
24	wedge
25	lodge
26	clear
27	coast
28	ring
29	run

Multiple meanings pp.31–32

30	spirit
31	rear
32	scrap
33	match
34	dash
35	sack
36	bold
37	wind
38	row
39	alert
40	pack
41	firm
42	hide
43	gloom
44	award
45	fan
46	lock
47	digit
48	tablet
49	spread
50	clear
51	rest
52	save
53	trip
54	instruct
55	hard
56	moped
57	excuse
58	lie
59	wound
60	back

Answers

1	A
2	A
3	C
4	C
5	D
6	B
7	A
8	C
9	D
10	B
11	C
12	C
13	D
14	A
15	D
16	B
17	C
18	C
19	B
20	D
21	A
22	C
23	B
24	C
25	B
26	B
27	D
28	D

29	A
30	D
31	C
32	D
33	A
34	D
35	B
36	D
37	C
38	B
39	D
40	B
41	D
42	C
43	C
44	A
45	B
46	A
47	D
48	C

Making words
pp.38–40

1	D	pageant
2	C	bargain
3	B	cargo
4	A	forehead
5	B	feather
6	D	island
7	C	legally
8	C	pantry
9	A	issue
10	B	offence
11	B	forage
12	D	heart
13	C	amenable
14	B	attempt
15	C	sealed
16	B	meant
17	C	referred
18	D	restrain
19	C	noon
20	D	armour
21	D	portray
22	B	template
23	B	moderate
24	B	rotate
25	D	rebellion
26	C	fortnight
27	D	pumpkin
28	D	poppies
29	B	soup
30	D	overturn

Making words
pp.41–42

31	B	theme
32	C	soon
33	C	washer
34	D	styled
35	B	allowed
36	D	modesty
37	C	reinvent
38	C	pleasure
39	B	discover
40	D	office
41	C	thanking
42	D	kindled
43	C	reappear
44	B	novice
45	C	carrot
46	B	tactless
47	D	stealthy
48	B	restart
49	B	another
50	B	archive

Verbal Reasoning

Answers

Cloze passages 1 & 2
p.43

1	F glance
2	C carpeted
3	H curios
4	A framed
5	E occupied
6	G lucky
7	B delicious
8	D fair
9	H read
10	E while

Cloze passages 3 & 4
p.44

1	D turned
2	A streets
3	G hazardous
4	B damage
5	J buckled
6	F creature
7	B prepared
8	G gathering
9	D meticulous
10	C curious

Cloze passages 5 & 6
p.45

1	G prised
2	B hollow
3	H five
4	D examine
5	F lying
6	D immense
7	B glance
8	G observing
9	A perspective
10	F perched

Cloze passages 7 & 8
p.46

1	F accompany
2	H thoughtfully
3	C hearty
4	E circular
5	B wafted
6	I bragged
7	C melodies
8	J cultivated
9	F fascination
10	A instrument

Cloze passages 9 & 10
p.47

1	E banks
2	B infested
3	G gnawed
4	A sugary
5	H squeaking
6	H brought
7	B piercing
8	E willing
9	C parting
10	F single

Cloze passages 11 & 12
p.48

1	C conjectured
2	H advanced
3	A houses
4	E inclined
5	F sounder
6	E terribly
7	J wretched
8	B irked
9	H focused
10	D decision

Shuffled sentences
pp.49–51

1	A
2	D
3	E
4	H
5	A
6	B
7	F
8	H
9	C
10	A
11	B
12	E
13	E
14	B
15	D
16	C
17	C
18	B
19	B
20	G
21	H
22	B
23	F
24	F
25	B
26	A
27	C
28	H
29	F
30	D

Shuffled sentences
pp.52–54

31	C
32	A
33	G
34	B
35	A
36	E
37	D
38	F
39	C
40	B
41	E
42	G
43	C
44	G
45	H
46	F
47	C
48	G
49	E
50	A
51	F
52	C
53	B
54	D
55	B
56	E
57	B
58	B
59	A
60	F

Notes

Notes